WHATCHA KNOW ABOUT THAT?:

URBAN POEMS AND SHORT STORIES

By: Heather Rutherford-Small

SMALL HOUSE PUBLISHING

Whatcha' Know About That?: Urban Poems and Short Stories

Small House Publishing
P.O. Box 1133, Live Oak, FL 32064 U.S.A.

Copyright © 2011 by Heather Rutherford-Small

All rights reserved. No part of this book may be reproduced or transmitted in any form or by any means, electronic or mechanical, including photocopying, recording, or by any information storage and retrieval system, without written permission from the author, except for the inclusion of brief quotations in a review.

Unattributed quotations are by Heather Rutherford-Small

International Standard Book Number

Softcover 978-0-98331-220-8

Printed in the United States of America

By Amazon

Library of Congress Cataloging-in-Publication Data
Rutherford-Small, Heather.
Whatcha' Know about That? : Urban Poems and Short Stories. C. 2011.
ISBN: 978-0-9833122-0-8
2011909633

Whatcha Know About That?

Preface   5

I. **Revealing**
- I'm Free   13
- Six Feet Away   15
- The Gang Trade   17
- Arrested Development   23
- For My Block   27
- Indecent Exposure   31
- Poisonous Snakes   35

II. **Dealing**
- This Thing Chose Me   41
- Memoirs of a Rapist   47
- Home Training   51
- What are your Investments?   55
- Replacing a 'Me' with 'We'   59
- Injustice   61
- Whatcha Know About That?   65

III. **Healing**
- Dear Heart   73
- Rules of the Game   77
- IF   79
- My Future   81
- Beauty Mark   83
- Stepping Into Your Future   85
- No One Taught Me   89

"If my people, which are called by my name, shall humble themselves, and pray, and seek my face, and turn from their wicked ways; then will I hear from heaven, and will forgive their sin, and will heal their land."

2 Chronicles 7: 14 (NIV)

Preface

My husband and I were in our 2007 ocean mist metallic blue Honda Odyssey, I in the driver's seat and he in the passenger's seat; when all of a sudden the van was inundated with a barrage of bullets from a 9mm machine handgun. After the initial shock of the incident I told my husband that I was getting out of the car to confront the guy who did this. As I reach toward the handle to open the door, my husband pleaded for me not to go; but there was something burning inside of me that I had to say. So, I proceeded to open the car door and yell for the guy to come to me, he turned and began to run away and then I felt compelled to call the gunman a rather unusual, and definitely a God inspired name. So, I sternly said "Israel," and the guy halted in his place and hesitantly began to turn around. I proceeded to say, "Israel, come here God has something He wants to say to you." At that point he began to come toward me with a curious expression on his face. As he approached me the ambiance changed from an eerie silence to the shriek of sirens. And I said to him, "God wants me to tell you that you are going to be a preacher." He looked at me with eyes filled with confusion and complete dumbfound; he replied "How can I be a preacher? I am about to go to prison." I responded, "Just because God calls you to be something today does not mean you will be that tomorrow, some things take time to manifest; you will still have to go to prison and serve your time but while you are there you can begin to grow yourself and do the work necessary to become what God has called you to be."

And with that final word the police surrounded the area, with guns drawn yelling "PUT YOUR HANDS UP!" The last image of this dream was the young man being placed in the police car with his hands behind his back.

I still have not made full sense of this dream yet, but what I did get out of it was a line to a poem. When I woke up from this dream a verse came to me that said "When the 5-0 came around the corner, I knew that shot meant that there would be mourners, once the officer called for the coroner." From this verse the seed was planted and grew into a poem titled "For My Block." This poem is the cornerstone and inspiration for this book. I wrote this poem after a culmination of the above dream as well as through the experiences that I had while mentoring and tutoring at a juvenile prison in Virginia. While working with the young men and women in the facility I learned more about their experiences than any textbook could have ever taught me.

I have always had a heart and passion for Religion, Psychology, and Criminal Justice; with a special interest in social justice. This book has given me a platform to express myself creatively about the issues facing our young people and those problems that need more attention. One key issue that deserves more consideration is Disproportionate Minority Confinement (DMC) as well as the realities and concerns of minority professionals in the field of Criminal Justice, not to mention the many other professions. With all the problems that our system faces, race should no longer be such a despairing issue. In my opinion our focus needs to be on educating and preparing the next generation for their inheritance of our future. We have to stop playing politics, stop talking about funding, and really begin to invest and attend to the needs of our children. This book tries to express some of the views that young urban youth face, through poetry and short stories. Many of the stories try to hone in on the perspectives of African American youth, though there are pieces that can apply to anyone. Regardless, of the piece's focus, everyone can learn something or at least try and experience life through someone else's eyes, if only for but a moment.

I stepped out on a limb for many of these pieces and I am cognizant of the fact that I am not qualified to speak on some of the events that I have written about. I am also clearly aware that I am a 27 year old white mother of two, who is a wife, and full time college student with tremendous audacity to attempt and express many of these events that I have not actually experienced. But, I have even greater faith in the God who placed these ideas and expressions in my mind and granted me the avenue to articulate them. I would not feel comfortable keeping these thoughts to myself and I do not believe they were given to me not to share them with others.

The spark that ignited the title of this book *"Whatcha Know About That?"* came from being asked several times what do I know about the lives of urban youth; meaning the struggles and dilemmas that urban adolescence face. As you read, you may want to ask me the same thing. So, with this acknowledgement I decided to, not only, make this the title of the book, but also to write a short story of the same title that flips the question back to young people. Asking them what do they know about their history, about the people who overcame seemingly insurmountable odds, about the fight that is still being fought, and about those who paid the ultimate for their freedoms and rights? At times it is necessary and probably essential to imagine what others go through and experience in order to progress and understand the necessary changes that must be implemented to make this life we live better, in every facet. So, with that being said, I hope you enjoy reading and experiencing this book as much as I did writing it!

Acknowledgements:

I have to give credit where credit is due, so first and foremost I thank God for all that He has done for me. I thank Him and His Son, my Lord and Savior Jesus Christ. His word is truly the lamp unto my feet and the light unto my path; by His grace, there go I.

Secondly, I cannot go without thanking my family. My supportive husband Eric, my children Eric Jr. and Elijah, my sister Christina, my parents, scores of extended family as well as friends who I consider family; have all in one way or another contributed to my current and future endeavors. Their love and sustenance has not gone unnoticed and I will be eternally grateful.

This book would not have been possible without the supportive and generative members of the National Association of Blacks in Criminal Justice (NABCJ). There are countless people in this organization that I consider mentors and friends. They have given me a platform to speak on and at times a microphone (very dangerous☺), which has blossomed a poem I wrote for the sake of expression, into the vary book you are now reading.

Lastly, my mentors, professors, and friends at Virginia Commonwealth University must be acknowledged. Without the experiences that have had at VCU and the hardworking passionate people there I would not have joined NABCJ which may have never led to this finished product. Their support and kindness is not overlooked!

"Behold, I will bring it health and cure, and I will cure them, and will reveal unto them the abundance of peace and truth."

Jeremiah 33: 6 (KJV)

Part I:

Revealing

But blessed is the one who trusts in the LORD, whose confidence is in him. They will be like a tree planted by the water that sends out its roots by the stream. It does not fear when heat comes; its leaves are always green. It has no worries in a year of drought and never fails to bear fruit. - Jeremiah 17:7-8 (NIV)

I'm Free

I'm free; I can go where ever I want to
I can hang out with whoever I want to
Because the company I keep doesn't affect me

I'm free, can't you see?

I'm free; I can do what I want to do
I can get high if I want to

Because I'm free can't you see I'm free!

I'm free; I can drink all I want
I can go and get drunk

Because I'm free, can't you see?

I'm free I can sleep with whoever I want to
I can have all the sex I choose to

Because I'm free can't you see?

I'm free I can go see what I want to see
Because seeing negative imagery has no effect on me

Don't you know I'm free, can't you see?

America tells us to let freedom ring
And we have taken this phrase too literally
We are the most free culturally
But we are bound spiritually and psychologically

Are we really free? I don't know you tell me...

Like one who takes away a garment on a cold day, or like vinegar poured on a wound, is one who sings songs to a heavy heart.

Proverbs 25: 20 (NIV)

Six Feet Away

I was six feet away from the door that I could have screamed out of

To get someone to come and show me some love

I was six feet away from the phone that I could have picked up

To see if someone was home to tell them I was alone

I was six feet from my notebook that I could have written in

I could have jotted down all of my problems but where would I begin?

I was six feet from the Bible that I got when I was young

I could have read of the man who had it worse than me and about the cross that He hung from

I was six feet away from the pill bottle that the doctors instructed me to take

So I opened them and took them I thought to take the pain away

I thought no one could understand the pain that I was going through

I lost faith in even my closest friends because I thought that they would fail me too

I was six feet from changing my mind I could have found another way

But it was easier for me to take those pills and take my life that day

I should have chose another path and it's too late to realize that now

I didn't know so many people loved me and I definitely couldn't see how

If I could say one last thing, this is what it would be

Taking your life is not the solution to your problems, just remember me

If you are in my situation and you feel there's no other way out

Just remember I was six feet away from life, but now I'm six feet underground.

In loving memory of TSP

The Gang Trade

Come on for a minute; if you will with me

I want to take you on a trip through history

Maybe it can open up your eyes so that you can see

All the things that you are doing no differently

You see there once was a time in America when there was slavery

When people owned Africans so that they could do all the work for free

There were boats, stolen lives, and a trade industry

That brought millions of people into involuntary custody

There was a master who owned slaves, and a crop to till

And the master made the slaves work against their will

They were bought, they were sold, and they were shuffled around

They were pushed; they were pulled, as their sweat beat the ground

There then came a time when the price for a slave was too much to pay

So the master rounded a male and female slave and a bed of hay for them to lay

You see they were treated worse than animals, so they had better take heed

Because the master had a need, for them to breed

A few hundred years ago there were slave men known as breeders

They were strong and worked hard so the master used them as womb seeders

They had numerous babies that they never had to care for

And so it seems the trend has continued and has circled around some more

Now we have babies having babies and too many kids being raised without their fathers

And the few who will step up to do their part need a DNA test before they'll even bother

Our young girls are selling their bodies to the highest paying John

But back on the plantation the girls were raped until their innocence was gone

It is clear their self esteem was stolen back in the slave quarters

Because today the girls give themselves away without establishing any standards or borders

If you ask me it's no different than slavery!

Now kids get "beat in" by choice, just for gang initiation

But if you look back at the slaves they were also beaten, if they could only see us now; could you imagine their frustration?

Today African Americans are herded into involuntary custody through incarceration

Stepping into an institution is like entering the slave trade which has stolen the promise of the future generations

The slaves worked to the bone to make their masters rich

They were raped, they were beaten, oh but here's the hitch

Today we live in a similar way

Because our youths voices have been silenced so we don't hear them say

That they need to be given the space for creative play

So, they choose various paths just so that they can survive

But these choices that they make don't always keep them alive

If you ask me it's no different than slavery!

We've gone from street gangs to chain gangs

We've gone from the slave trade to the gang trade

The echo of guns that are clicked and fired off

Resemble the sounds of the whips that were too often cracked and popped

The knives that are now used in robberies leave long and bleeding gashes

And the marks that are left look like the backs of the slaves that were littered with leather imprinted lashes

The gangs kill each other off because of the colors that they wear

But the Africans had no choice in their skin color and so their skin was their cross to bear

Now the kids use graffiti to mark their territory

And the symbols that they use are supposed to tell their story

But the slaves left their own signs that should not be so easily overlooked

Because this gang thing is the new slave trade and our kids have been baited and hooked

Like cattle the slaves were branded so the master could identify which ones were his possessions

We know that the love of money is the root of all kinds of evil and so this greed has turned into an obsession

They would be categorized and branded with rods of iron that were blistering hot

But fraternities and gangs also use brands today, because it is clear that they have forgot

About the ones who lived so long ago in such horrible conditions

Who were tortured relentlessly and whose worst fears have come into fruition

Because they wanted better for the following generations and they never wanted their pain to be forgotten

But it is clear that we have fallen back into old traps and that too many people have now bought in

To Satan's lies and in his grasp so many have gotten caught in

So, it is now time to wake up, get loose, and let real freedom ring

Because right now the chain gangs are singing the odes that the slaves used to sing

But we have this treasure in jars of clay to show that this all-surpassing power is from God and not from us. [8] We are hard pressed on every side, but not crushed; perplexed, but not in despair; [9] persecuted, but not abandoned; struck down, but not destroyed.

I Corinthians 4: 7-9 (NIV)

Arrested Development

Now that it's the weekend, it is time to hit the road

But the small car that we travel in isn't big enough to haul this load

The highway is always way to long, the wait is much too much

I hate having to be put through this every few months just to feel your touch

I'll never forget the day that you had to leave I felt so confused

It felt like my heart was crushed, it left my spirit bruised

Grandma told me to sit down, right as I walked in from getting off the school bus

She said, "I have something to tell you about your momma, but don't you start to fuss."

She continued to say that you had to go away for awhile so that you could get some help

She also said that we must keep this private which left me with no one that I could tell

I am angry that you left us; I am saddened that you are gone

I cannot help but feel as though I've done something wrong

It feels like no one wants me, as though I'm a burden on the world

This pain is too much to bear for any little boy or girl

Why do I have to grow up without you?
Why did the police have to take you away?
Why am I the one who is left alone?
Why is this, the price that I must pay?

Why do I have to come to this cold concrete place, just to hear your voice, and to see your face?

Most kids don't have to talk to their moms by telephone or through letters

Which I have kept hidden away in a box as though they are my secret treasures

You tell me that I need to listen to my grandma and that I must do whatever she may say

But you didn't listen or obey because if you did then they wouldn't have taken you away

So why should I listen? Disobedience is my plea for help, it's the only thing I know

I don't know how to articulate my thoughts so my angry feelings must be shown

I feel so ashamed to have to hide this but what other choice do I have

Maybe if I could tell others that my parents are gone to war instead of prison then it wouldn't feel so bad

Whatcha Know About That? | 25

I don't know what to think, I feel so confused

Because even as mad as I am, I still really love you

What will people think of me, what do they think of you?

I can't risk my chances at a normal life; I don't want anyone else to know the truth.

So, when the other kids ask to come over to play I always make up an excuse that will suffice

This is what I have to give up from my childhood, this is what I sacrifice

I tell them that I have to stay with my grandma a lot, especially on the weekends

I want so bad to tell them the truth, but where would I begin?

These excuses have worked so far now but they won't last too much more

Soon I'll begin to get the questions about why you don't show up to anything......
God why do I have to do this for?

The statistics say that I'm likely to end up just like you

They say that I am an "at risk" child who will probably end up incarcerated too

Do you know what you have done to me, what you've set me up for?

The only money we have is granny's social security check because there is not funding for this type of poor

The odds are growing rapidly against me and the time will one day come

When I have to choose between making a life of my own or to stick to the one that I've come from

I am meant to be so much more than the example you've shown, I know my purpose in life is more than what you have become

I'm gonna do some things different to live my life right

I'm gonna start to pray and I'm gonna start tonight

Because God is the only one who will fix this mess that you've put me in

So I'm gonna trust in Him to show me His way so that my successful beginning won't meet your end

For My Block

I was born into the colors of my family
A life that seemed deemed for struggle and poverty
But this is part of my lineage and my legacy
So, as soon as I hit puberty

I had to make a choice

The day comes for me to be initiated
And now the hook was set and I was baited
And as I sat on the corner and waited
Myself and I debated

When the prey came focused in my scope, I wonder did I make the right choice

It is too late for all of that now the plan was already set. And as my hand began to sweat
With my finger on the trigger I knew I wasn't ready yet

But this task I must complete, if I want to prove that I am holdin' it down for my street

So, I aimed the barrel with a cock because this was for my block

After the shot rang out, I froze; because the body the bullet chose

Was not one of our rivals so, I began to plead for the victim's survival

But when the 5-0 came around the corner
I knew the shot meant there would be mourners
Once the officer called for the coroner

I couldn't move but my mind was runnin'
And all I could do was stand there stunnin'

Then I began to envision
How I could change this decision
But this thought quickly ended

With cold metal wrapping around my wrist
Then suddenly my cheek was kissed by a fist
Because the boys brother was pissed

And as they read my rights to me
The only thing my mind could see
Was the funeral plans being made by the boy's family

I missed my target; it had never gone down like this
before. And as the news resonated in my core
I remembered what I did it for

And the only thing I knew, is that I still had my crew

And I did it all for my block

At the funeral they read Psalms 23
Around the same time that they indicted me
And the future as far as I could see

Was over....

The judge and the preacher in synchrony
Said I need to hear a testimony
And as the stories were told in harmony
One ended in praise, the other in penalty

They then both asked if they could get a witness
As the judge requested a test of my mental fitness

He then ruled that I be transferred

Because of all the evidence that he had heard
And both the church and the court ended with a final word

And as I stood there shaking
The verdict was in the making
Which concluded with two lives taken

When his casket closed, so did my cell
And, I knew I had just entered hell
And I caused the same for his family as well

But I did it for my block

Now I am 15 convicted as an adult with a life sentence
 I sit here each day and pray for repentance
Yet, my mind is always reminiscent

Of the days on my block

No one comes to see me anymore
And as the memories they fade
So does the flowers on his grave
Two lives seemed to end in a heartbeat
And it seems they were both extinguished in defeat
Because it was all only for my street

You see, innocent people are dying
And their families are crying
With too many kids who buy in
To the OGs that are lying

About a fantasy that will never be
A promised life of prosperity
But we all know there ain't nothing for free
Because I did something for them, that they wouldn't do for me
Now, I am here for what seems like eternity

And that is fair because death is also forever

And sometimes I just wonder if I was born through the wrong womb
Because everything in my life has been doomed
And everything good seems to have been consumed
In this raging fire that has always loomed

And now the racists who have hated us have won their victory
Because we no longer need to be hung from a tree
We kill each other now you see
And it is all for the sake of belonging to our street's family

The only way things are going to change
Is for our thinking to be rearranged

Stop thinking that you have to kill or be killed
Spill blood for blood spilled
Take it to make it
Mug or be mugged

Instead we should try
Loving to be loved
Hugging to be hugged

And at the end of the day
When we make it we can say
That something good came from all of our pain
And all the work we did to change

Was all for our block....

(written: April 29, 2010)

Indecent Exposure:

I am writing this now with a heart that is heavy
It feels like a 2005 New Orleanian levee

The floodgates are about to break and the truth will overflow
There is no telling where this ode is going to go

I can no longer keep quiet about the injustices I see
My conscience will not let me continue to proceed silently

You have to see that our voices are muted so that our frustration will build, hoping that a stereotypic response it will yield

To perpetuate the ignorance to be passed down from one generation to the next, making people feel alienated and accept only second best.

Getting second rate schools, and second hand books, hand me down facilities but never second looks

We pay taxes and levies just like the next city but our kids are treated like lepers who are never touched and only shown pity

They say…. "Oh it is so sad, those kids over there, who live off the government for food, clothes, shelter, and healthcare"

What child ever decided to be born into this mess?
Why are they the ones who have the burden of passing our tests?

Why are the things that they need, and the
importance of their voices
Always being silenced and why are they held
accountable for their parents poor choices

"We're sorry little Jonny that you live in section 8
housing, that you can't afford school supplies, and
that your dad didn't find your mom worth spousing."

We'll hold you responsible! And you better pay up,
You'll pay through your future and your education
and you'll be the one who is left holding the cup

Yes this cup once held coffee for a rich CEO
But now you will hold it, with a sign that goes like so:

"Please help me, I'm homeless, I have nothing to eat
I'm paying for my inherited sins by having to live on
the street."

So, what's the solution you now may be asking?
Is it money, is it power, is it committees built for
tasking?

Should we continue to throw money at an ever
growing problem?
Expecting Grant, Jefferson, and Ben Franklin to solve
them?

Funding is not the issue, and it really never has been
Would you take a nickel for a headache or swallow an
aspirin?

Just because you have a seed doesn't mean that you'll
reap it and just because you have a book doesn't
mean you can read it

Our policies and legislations are far above the children's heads but the choppy waters of our regulations is the cesspool that they must tread

And if they cannot keep up then they surely will drown
And the "well of perpetual poverty" is on the one they will have to throw their buckets down

This system has been built that one can never get out once they're in and in order to start a new life they literally have to be born again

Because the day they decide that they will make their own way the price for their independence is too steep to pay

You see if Kimmie decides that she wants to get a legitimate job that will suffice, all the previous assistance she had she must now sacrifice

She will lose her health coverage and the childcare for the kids, she will have a reduction in food stamps so it's now time to sink or swim

The only problem with this picture is that she has been given no instructions
So her pathway is doomed, she's been set up for destruction

So what do we do? How do we fix this nightmare? Where do we begin, what lessons must be shared?

Even though truth can be difficult, the starting point is not blaming someone else
Own up to what you are responsible for and begin improving yourself

The solution is quite simple and it really always has been
This same little secret is what has always worked to make something happen

See when your mind starts wandering down this troublesome slope
The only thing to be done is to rebuild your hope

Because once your hope is restored there is no telling what breakthroughs can be made
All of the dreams that you have let go of can once again be saved

Let's take back our possibilities, our talents, and our power
Let go of the unchangeable and attend to this critical hour

Because one stone thrown into a pond has a rippling effect
And the future can be changed by what we choose to do next

You see the only thing that we have that no one can ever take
Are the things that we know and the choices that we make

So, as angry and frustrating as this situation may be
Remember that it is your choices that ultimately determine your destiny

Poisonous Snakes:

Looking around the smoke filled room I observe many lives that have been stolen. Their minds have been taken by a poison, a poison that creeps through the body while corrupting the thoughts of a normally well-rounded person. The stench of cheap cigarettes engulfs my lungs which expedites my departure, but I stay for a few more minutes if only to get a sign or an understanding of why. Why would anyone surround the life they've been given with immediate pleasures that profit them nothing?

As I sit in the corner; almost as if I was observing from the outside looking in, I ponder with my fists to my cheeks and my elbows on the table. I see a lady in a skimpy skirt, very pretty, but disturbed. I think to myself, what is going on in her life? Why is she working here to make ends meet? The men tap her and ask for more venom to fill their bellies and she thinks nothing of it as she goes to the bar and leaves the order for another shot. As most of them, the snakes say, "Just one more shot," or "This will be the last time." But is it really? The wives of these men have given up on the "One last times," and the "I promise I'll stop." They are at home with lost hopes of a knight in shining armor because all they got was a sloppy drunk.

I leave because overwhelming thoughts rush in that I could no longer tolerate. I walked out and decided to go to the store on my way home. As I walk down the sidewalk smelling the foul smells of the city, I see four women. They have their hair done up and their nails done too, with cigarettes in hand because the poison has stolen them too. They have on short skirts, showing as much as they can reveal, with their breasts perked just right to catch the eye of a passerby who is looking for some cheap sex tonight. Then the thoughts come rushing back again of why. Why would they sell their beautiful bodies to men who care nothing for them? Just for money? Just for a place to live? Just for another fix?

    I continue walking to my destination, and as I come closer to the corner store, I see a man on a bench. He is there, waiting for his next dose. I try not to assume things but I see him there almost every night. And as his poison provider comes, they maneuver in such slyness that is it hard to determine that they are really doing a deal. But it is obvious when the addict comes around from the back of the store ten minutes later with slurred speech, dilated pupils, and laughing at nothing. Well something, but only he can see it. As the poison flows through his body and gives him images of objects that aren't even there, he laughs. Here they come again, these thoughts. Do we really need to destroy our entire lives just to make us laugh for ten minutes? Do we really need to give up all we have worked for because of a void that needs to be filled? I don't understand why we choose pacification over patience. I know it is easier that way, at least initially, but is it really? Easier to get through the day, but when all is said and done what do we really live for?

    As I continue on my journey, I come to the door of the store. I open the door and proceed to go in to get a pack of gum and a soda. As I reach the freezer handle to open it, I hear a deep voice demanding, "Give me all the money in the drawer, or I'll shoot you in your f***ing head," as if he didn't know anyone else was in the store. I assume he didn't see me, so I slowly sit down with my back to the freezer before he had the chance to notice me. I can see very little, only the corner of the robbers pant leg with his seemingly new sneakers, from behind the potato chip aisle. I take a deep breath and get ready to run as soon as the robber leaves, and as soon as I know that he has gotten away, I get up and l hastily exit the store. When I get outside, I can hear the screams of the sirens come closer, it seems that the pigs always show up just a little too late. I guess that is because some pigs are afraid of snakes. As I get about a block away from the store, I regain my composure and begin to head home. As I walk I begin to recollect the well known Bible verse that says, 'the love of money is the root of all kinds of evil.' After tonight, I begin to see the truth in that statement.

    I can't believe this is a regular occurrence; this stuff happens every night almost in synchronized fashion. It almost seems as if people look forward to waking up and hearing on the six o'clock morning news of what went down the night before. Who did the drunk driver kill, what prostitute was murdered, what addict went crazy, and what store was robbed? While recalling all these things, I don't remember the rest of the walk home. All I can remember is coming to my door, and putting the key in to unlock it. Once I get in I sit my keys down on the coffee table. I try to relax from the stressful events that I witnessed that evening, so I sit in my lounge chair and turn on the T.V. and there I realize that I also need some poison to get me through the night as well.

25 And I will restore to you the years that the locust hath eaten, the cankerworm, and the caterpillar, and the palmerworm, my great army which I sent among you.

26 And ye shall eat in plenty, and be satisfied, and praise the name of the LORD your God, that hath dealt wondrously with you: and my people shall never be ashamed.

27 And ye shall know that I am in the midst of Israel, and that I am the LORD your God, and none else: and my people shall never be ashamed.

Joel 2: 25-17 (KJV)

**Part II:
Dealing:**

My kinsfolk have failed, and my familiar friends have forgotten me.

Job 19: 14 (KJV)

This Thing Chose Me:

You know we're wheeling and dealing and we're making a killing

And as the money piles up so do the souls that we're stealing

Yeah we run this street without skipping a beat

But, if I had another choice I'd gladly give up this seat

Some say we should have chosen a different way to be

But deciding between life and death is not really a choice to me

I didn't ask to go to bed each night to the sounds of sirens

Or to the clicks and the 'pop, pop. pop's because of the guns that are always firing

I didn't ask to be robbed for the shoes on my feet

And I sure as hell didn't asked to be born and raised on this God forsaken street

I used to have dreams when I was a little kid about the things that I could do

But all those things quickly changed after a few years of going to school

I thought that I would know how to read and learn many new things

But my imagination has been starved and my mind has hunger pangs

The teachers have lost their focus because of dealing with us kids

So they begin to see us all the same, as a pest that they must rid

They keep pushing us through grade after grade because they get sick of seeing our faces

They just wish that they could teach us what they know and not have to take our parents places

And so this cycle continues to circle around child after child

And then they have the nerve to say we shouldn't look so sad and that we should wear a smile

Many of us kids don't know our dads and this story is a shame

But on top of that our moms have lied to us about the 'uncles' who have gone and came

Growing up in a world where no one wants you and treats you like you are trash

Is the check that has been written to me, but this check I don't want to cash

You keep telling me that I've failed, but really I think it is you who have failed me

Because a child should not have to choose between love and family

I've been in and out of juvenile homes and this part gets really sad

Because people treated me better in there than anyone out here has ever had

I was fed 3 meals a day and I knew where I would sleep

I had counselors who I could talk to and trust that my secrets they would keep

I was complimented for the first time ever and at first I took offense

You see, no one had ever said anything nice to me before without it having an expense

So as much as I would like to prove you right and say that this was my bad decision

I have to believe this thing chose me and that this is the life that I have been given

...

But now that I've come to recognize how these things have happened to me

I am now responsible for making better choices from here on out to make my life what I want it to be

Those things in my past I may not have chosen but today the choice is mine

To step out and start to make the necessary changes so that I can be just fine

I am realizing that now I may not have been able to control the things that happened in the past

But now I have full control of my future, the choice is mine; at last!

Now why dost thou cry out aloud? is there no king in thee? is thy counsellor perished? for pangs have taken thee as a woman in travail.
Micah 4: 9 (KJV)

But he refused to listen to her, and since he was stronger than she, he raped her.
2 Samuel 13: 14 (NIV)

Memoirs of a Rapist

Everything you know about me you read in a manila folder
You think you know who I am because of what someone else has told ya

And as the papers in my file continue to stack up
the charges that I built persistently rack up
and while this hole that I'm digging gets deeper I'm making it harder for myself to ever get back up

The truth of the matter is my story is too raw and real.
What I have been through has made my heart too numb to feel

The things that they said that I have done, I cannot even believe
But as much as I want to fight the accusations, the DNA points straight to me

I have been rejected so many times in life that "NO" meant nothing to me.
And from a young age I learned if I wanted something I take it because dismissal has been the only result I ever seem to see.

So if she really told me no, my ears were deaf to hear
Because my ego wouldn't handle anymore rejection so her requests never came in clear

What about all those other girls who had also declined my advances
They never prosecuted me; they all just gave me second chances

I never thought what I did was wrong, I thought it was something that I was owed

It was about time that I got something and for some
reverence to be shown

You see I have no control over anything; my life, my
kids, my job
So it came to be that I had to take over something,
even if it meant that it was innocence that I robbed.

Okay, come on now, let me be real; I knew all along
what I had done was wrong
But, I had to disguise all of my weaknesses so this
was my façade at being strong

You see I've told myself I didn't do it so many times
that I began to believe in my own lies.

I tuned out those women and their cries
I ignored their pain and unsuccessful tries,

To escape my fury, to flee my wrath
To try and get away unscathed, to avoid my traps

They might have fought, and they might have flailed
They may have struggled and they may have wailed
And the saddest part of this whole tale, is that they all
tried to stand up for themselves, but they failed

I became a victor through creating victims
I took control of their bodies and their clothes and I
ripped'em

I took from them more than I would have ever known
Because most of the scars they are left with are ones
that could never be shown

The one who pressed charges was the only one who
had ever challenged my behavior
I guess you could say that she was a hero because she
was my prospective target's savior

I can't say that I don't deserve to be here, but man
this is an awful life to live
I wish I had found a better outlet for my aggression
and a way to forgive

If I had it to do all over I would have chosen another
way
But it's too late for all of that so before I end there is
one last thing I have to say
If being locked up has taught me anything about what
my victims went through it is feeling what it is like to
be someone else's prey

Whosoever findeth a wife findeth a good thing, and obtaineth favour of the LORD.

Proverbs 18: 22 (KJV)

Home Training:

There is a phenomenon occurring and many people are complaining

About what they say our generation lacks and they call this thing "home training"

Our standards have been misplaced because we live in a world that says "you gotta have it now"

We have lost the virtues of work ethic and to the god of materialism, we now bow

Our expectations for results have exponentially increased

But the time and effort we put into securing those things, have just as equally become deceased

Some think they have all the benefits of a marriage without needing to have a spouse

They think they are taking a part in the profits, without the commitment. This masquerade is called "playing house."

And the bills are being racked up while this new couple shacks up

The only thing that is growing is a whole lot of debt which turns into anger and eventually regret

And the woman thinks to herself, 'Oh, I know he'll marry me someday, yes I believe it's true, but in the mean time I'll continue to do all things a wife is supposed to do."

And the man has a thought that is very much different from hers "Why should I get married now I get all the perks of a wife without marriage, I'm not giving up my bachelorhood."

And because they don't know each other's true desires they won't keep up their 'Fruit of the Looms'

And eventually they end up producing 'Fruit of the Womb'

And one day this fruit will be in full bloom

And based on current statistics, it shows that the baby is doomed

And after the seed has fully grown and the labor is done

There remains God's gift of a daughter or son

And the seeds that have been sown

Someday will be grown

And as history has shown

The kids will grow up to do the same thing because it is all they have known

As the saying goes, "the fruit doesn't fall very far from the tree."

So this unsuspecting baby repeats history

Because they think that this dilemma won't catch them up too

They think that they are different, invincible.... even bulletproof

So, they take the same risks that their parents once took

And it is awfully sad because they too will be on the hook

For a baby and broken dreams of a better tomorrow

All that is left from this mess is a whole lot of sorrow

We have to take Ghandi's advice and be the change we want to see

Stop duplicating this cycle; it's time to break free

We have to make better choices and take control of our destiny

And instead of repeating it... let's make history!

Each of you should use whatever gift you have received to serve others, as faithful stewards of God's grace in its various forms.

1 Peter 4:10 (KJV)

What are your investments?

Many people wonder why they just can't get ahead

They keep trying to move forward but go in reverse instead

I ask you now to take a minute, and to contemplate

Focus on what is being asked of you before it becomes too late

Now really think hard about where you are putting your potential

Is it your work, your family, your faith, your credentials?

What is it that you spend most of your time doing?

Is it in creative production or is it in resentfully stewing

Are you content with the returns that you are getting from what you invest?

Are the things that you are gathering matching what you've seeded for harvest?

Now take a look at it this way, it may help you to see

That everything in life works like a garden; we'll call it a money tree

You know you only get what you put in; yeah you reap what you sow

If you leave no deposited seeds then nothing will ever grow

If you go to a bank to make a withdrawal without having a balance in your account

Then "insufficient funds" is the message you'll get and the check you just wrote will bounce

You cannot get water out of a well unless the water supply is ample

Thus, many aspects of your life can work this way let me give you some examples

Let's first take a look at the family, if this is where your returns lack

Maybe you can begin to see why you feel shorted and why you aren't getting much back

Reminisce for a second on the time you've invested in the members you are upset about

When was the last time you took part in an interest of theirs without acting like it put you out?

Have you really invested the loving care that it takes to nurture a genuine bond?

Or have you just gone through the motions with them and expected them to lovingly respond?

If it is an intimate relationship that you are longing for or one you wish to work out

Whatcha Know About That? | 57

Here are a few things to consider yes, some things to think about

I am sure that you have compiled a mental list of all the things your dream partner should be

The features they should have, their position and status, and about how they should be debt free

All these things you want in a partner; their success and ensuring that they are stable

Are all fine and good, but let me ask you about the assets you are bringing to the table,

Because the lover you desire has a similar list, in which they expect their partner to fulfill

Don't come to the drawing board with a hefty supply list, unless you can equally foot the bill

You see every time things turn into a liability it becomes a pain in your assets

The more you rely on someone else to make a way the deeper you go indebt

Stop sitting on the sideline, pointing fingers, and making up explanations

Don't complain any longer about your current status and quit coming up with justifications

It is time to get your hands dirty to get what you have always desired

Be patient and you'll see the seeds begin to grow, and this will keep you inspired

Start building a nest egg now so that your provisions have somewhere to lie down

And as all these things begin to develop you will see your situation turning around

As long as you keep doing what you have always done you will continue to get the same balance

If you want to see your endowments grow you have to employ all of your talents

Don't let your vision be tainted with wishes of a quick fix

Because things that come easily can be just as easily dismissed

It is time now to create a plan of action, do not let your plan become corrupted

Because anything that is not labored for will only leave you feeling depleted and bankrupted

So, I leave you now with this final thought of how these changes you can begin to implement

No matter the tangibility of the things you desire; start paying attention to how and where your investments are being spent.

Replacing a 'Me' with 'We'

We live in a time that has taken the 'I' in identity way too seriously

We have embraced the 'I' in individual and applied it literally

We have found the "me" in awesome and the "own" in shown

We have enjoyed the "me" in some and the "own" in grown

...

The problem with this all is that we have taken far too much individual credit

All these things could not be without another and we have made every attempt to forget it

Of course it sounds nice to be responsible for our successes and triumphs

But, we cannot leave out the ones who have sacrificed just to make a way for us

We have to begin to reconnect all the pieces that make us who we are

Stop being so self-absorbed and start resetting the metaphorical bar

You see no one is an island; we are all parts to a whole

We cannot take all the acknowledgment without losing part of our soul

Because once you take the 'me' out of some all you are left with is 'so'

And the faster this is recognized then the faster we will grow

Because even in the face of the bright lights, a shadow is standing behind

And once we realize all of our support is in the ones who lie in the shadows then true victory is what we'll find

When we can see the we in well

Then we can begin to finally heal

By putting back the 'we' into awesome and the 'us' in trust

We can slowly get rid of our passionate anger and overlook the 'us' in bust

After all these steps are taken we may remember the we in well-doing

We can enjoy each other for our differences and strengths and a much improved future we can together begin pursuing

Injustice

My heart is pounding, palms sweating, waiting impatiently for the judge to spit out her already decided verdict. There is nothing left to do or say but wait, and the seconds feel like minutes. Why am I here, I'm not a criminal? What did I do, I haven't killed anyone, robbed anyone, or raped anyone? Yet, when the arbitrator declares the sentence it screams through my body and wakes up my bones, and all I want to do is shatter something. I can't believe this is happening to me! I love my daughter I would never hurt her; I only want the best for her! So why, I'm trying, I'm doing the best I can do, I just found a good job, but now I'll lose that too.

When you get caught up in the system there is no way out, it is a never ending cycle that will stick with you for the rest of your life! And they wonder why we can't make it, they wonder why we don't have jobs, they wonder why we just can't seem to get our lives straight. Ha! It is a joke, court date after court date, and all unfair trials. I don't like to make the excuse of discrimination but today it was blatantly obvious. Before the trial the white witch walks in and has a friendly conversation with the judge, because she is a friend of the family! Huh? What is this; it is a mockery of the judicial system!

I thought this was the land of the free. it is land of the free, the land of the free white man. When you walk into a jail it is like stepping into Africa, it looks that way, though they took the African out of us. How can this be allowed, they say "equal rights," but I don't see it, it is just something that sounds good on paper. If you look at the truth this great war is still being fought. You say you want the truth but the truth you cannot handle. You say you want a deeper understanding of why we act this way, but do you really?

If anyone can get out of the system after being put in it, it is only by the hand of God Himself! They want us to get back on the right track after being released but when you have to lie to get a job, and you have to sneak your way through just to find a place to live, do they really mean it? Eventually the boss man will find out, and the landlord too and then I'm left again with no job and no place to live, which will put me back in jail because child support doesn't grow on trees.

Don't make a mistake when you are young, especially if you are a minority, there is no room for mistakes here. You get caught up and you can't get free. It is like being a delicate fish in a big pool of hungry sharks; they are out to get you. At least that is what it feels like, they don't know where I came from, they don't know what I have seen, and when each of them beat down on you time after time eventually you begin to think that it is an agenda of the white man.

Then they expect us to like them, not to mention be polite to them, "treat them with respect." They don't want us to fight back or retaliate because in that case when we do we are labeled as 'n*****s.' Sure there are ignorant people out there, to get technical; no one seems to look at the real definition of n****r. And treating someone unfairly because you won't take time to know them is ignorance to me.

It wouldn't make me so mad if I wasn't trying and if I didn't think the world of my child. I would do anything for my daughter. They make it seem like I don't love her and that I don't want to support her. The judge wouldn't even hear my side, I guess because she already has her mind made up about us. It is just so backwards, and now I'll have to spend six months in jail without seeing my child. When I get out all I've worked for will be gone and I will have to start all over again. Good thing I have faith in God because I would have killed myself by now if I didn't. I know He has a purpose for this, of course I haven't been perfect, but I'm honest and I'm dedicated. With Him I can do anything, and I know with Him justice will always prevail. Here I am justifying why I'm not supposed to be in this position which shouldn't be the case.

"Put your hands behind your back," declares the bailiff and then and there I fully recognize that today injustice was served.

For I do not want you to be ignorant of the fact, brothers and sisters, that our ancestors were all under the cloud and that they all passed through the sea.

1 Corinthians 10: 1 (KJV)

Whatcha Know About That?

     One night after watching a documentary on the rise of gangs in America, I began to think about why this phenomenon is occurring. I mean, I know the typical analysis leads many to believe that gangs are on the rise because these kids are ultimately looking for family, acceptance, and most importantly protection. But, there has to be more to it than that, there must be an underlying issue that has escaped these youth. There has to be a disconnection between history and the situation we have found ourselves in today. And as I begin to develop a theory it occurs to me; these kids don't know where they came from! I have to believe if they knew their histories then it would change some of their present lifestyle choices. And that this hasn't just occurred with their generation but also with generations previous to theirs.

     They talked about drive-bys on the documentary and how these kids shoot up people as they sit in a car. But, if I asked them what a "sit-in" really was they have no clue what I am talking about. If I asked them about Black History Month they can recall Dr. King. But when I say what about his "Letter from a Birmingham Jail," or his dream they just shrug their shoulders. The kids say that no one can understand their reality or their truth but what about Sojourner and her Truth? They talk about fighting a war on the streets to keep their block secure but when I ask them about the black soldiers who fought in the Civil War, they make a mockery of the soldiers heroism and sacrifice along with the freedom that they died for. There is a lot of talk about the underground drug smuggling operations that in many ways funds these gangs, but if I asked them about Harriet Tubman's Underground Railroad and the pathways she made to free hundreds of slaves they cannot comment. Young people gladly sit in the back of the classroom because they are too preoccupied with their lives to pay attention and be productive in the front, but they fail to realize that at one time black people were made to sit in the back, and that Rosa Parks along with many others fought for their right to sit in the front. They drop out of school and consume themselves full time on their criminal activity because apparently it has proven to be more profitable for them than an education. But, I mention Frederick Douglass and his determination to educate and free all slaves and they can only question "is that the man with the long white hair? They would post his picture up during Black History Month in the halls at school, well that is all I remember about him when I actually went to school anyway." I proceed to question them because I needed a sign that they knew something of our history, something about what we went through.

I decide to take a walk so that I could ponder these internal questions. I begin to observe the graffiti covered walls around me and I ask the next young person that passes by about the myriad of colors that I see on the buildings. He basically said that the kids paint up these walls as a way to mark their territory; and that they can disrespect another gang by painting over their signs and symbols and that it is a way for them to show "who owns this street." I shake my head and say, "what do you know about the KKK? Did you know that they too used to mark their territory they would terrorize and burn down the homes and churches of black people, they would set crosses on fire in the yards of anyone who supported the progression of black people, and that they used to decorate the limbs of the trees with the nooses and the necks of their most unfortunate victims who were caught up in their wrath? Then they would leave the bodies hanging there for a few days as a symbol to warn others of their fate if they dared to get in the way"

  I listen intently on the excuses they make for why they feel they have to participate in such nonsense. Why they feel secure in their decisions to kill each other for no other reason but that the other threw up the wrong sign, or wore the wrong color. Many live by such expressions like "I'll ride or die for mine," but they haven't been educated on those that have already laid their lives down and paid the ultimate sacrifice for them to live a better life. They have forgotten, and sadly may have never heard of, the many first African Americans who paved the way before them. These kids have been hypnotized by the material things this world has to offer and they have sold their souls to the Devil just to obtain them. But the question I am left with is, "What does it profit a man to gain the whole world, but lose his soul?"

  It is clear that they never learned that at one time when all else failed and when there seemed no way through, we prayed. That is right, that is how the slaves made it through the hellish boat ride and that is how they endured the sweat on their brow and the lashes on their backs. That is how they survived the loss of everything they knew, everything they owned, and everything they hoped to be. That is how they escaped, how they gained freedom, and how they made a way to survive after slavery. There was constantly a prayer in their song, a prayer in their labor, and a prayer in their heart. Black people for centuries have prayed their way through to see the sunshine during the gloomiest days. They have prayed to be free, prayed to be educated, prayed to be integrated, prayed to be equal, prayed to be humanized, prayed to survive, prayed to endure the consequences of their stance, and prayed for the ability to keep on praying. And, as I recall all this it becomes clear to me that somewhere between the Civil Rights Movement and now we have forgotten to pray. One of the key Bible verses that for many Christians has become a verse they live by, is 2 Chronicles 7:14 that says "if my people, who are called by my name, will humble themselves and pray and seek my face and turn from their wicked ways, then will I hear from heaven and will forgive their sin and will heal their land." And, because we have failed to humble ourselves and stand naked before the Lord our God, our land is suffering, it is plagued by violence, theft, hunger, poverty, anger, hatred, lust, greed, and all of the other sins that make us have to endure such struggles, as we do now. This generation has fallen prey to the traps that Satan has set, and all we have done is set back and watched them.

We have fought for freedom so strongly that we forgot how we made it and in turn we forgot that God was who brought us through. We lost focus and it seems we have begun to think that we were solely responsible for making our own way. Well, you can clearly see the repercussions of that kind of thinking. As long as we give ourselves all the credit for our progress and forget to thank God we will continue to see the true limitations of humans. As long as we continue to set God aside as a tool that was only used during those times, and fail to see how He is still relevant and has always been the same God, we will continue to see failure. As long as we put limitations on God by implying that He is only good for certain circumstances but He can't handle current ones then we will continue to see our people face seemingly insurmountable obstacles. God will only be to us as big as we allow Him to be, if we think that God can only help here but not there then that is exactly what we will see of Him. If we have faith that the God who created us can also do exceedingly, abundantly, and above all that we ask for then we can begin to accurately realize and appreciate the strides that our ancestors have made. We must begin to understand the importance of education, prayer, and teaching each generation about the history that preceded them. If we don't we will continue to lose the hope of the future that we have in our youth.

In hopes of getting a reasonable response I ask one more question. I inquire another young person about Malcolm X and what he stood for and they made a comment about Denzel being on point in that movie. At that point I am disheartened and honestly discouraged and I then recite this quote from a great figure in the Civil Rights Movement, that said:

"My hope for the next generation is for them to do better then what we have done. Make sure the children know their history so that they can fully embrace all that the future has to offer them. Teach them and love them. Let the innocence of their youth not only help them learn about where they came from, but also help them to have the faith to forgive so that we can all move on into an era of compassion for humanity as opposed to being broken down by a history of oppression."

The Spirit of the Lord is upon me, because he hath anointed me to preach the gospel to the poor; he hath sent me to heal the brokenhearted, to preach deliverance to the captives, and recovering of sight to the blind, to set at liberty them that are bruised,

Luke 4: 18 (KJV)

**Part III:
Healing**

Create in me a pure heart, O God,
and renew a steadfast spirit within me

Psalms 51: 10 (KJV)

Dear Heart:

Dear Heart,

Confronting you is one of the hardest things to do. Convincing others of what I go through is easy because a quick smile and an "I'm alright" will send them on their way. But you; you care. You are my passion, my energy, my love source. You help me see beyond faults, beyond fears, and you are honest with me. You give me strength to say caring things, to tell others the truth, and to do the right thing in spite of the situation I may be placed in.

There is a part of you that God needs to clean out, a place that only He can heal, it is the love spot. And if you don't let Him heal you then bitterness and hatred will take over. All of the many things that you have gone through we need to work out, all the hurt, all the shame, all the things that are keeping you from pumping passion like you used to. No matter how tough things get we have to take a step back and look at what is really going on so that I can help plan to make things brighter for us.

We must remember what keeps you warm, because there are too many people with cold hearts that just merely pump blood through their mundane veins. There is no room for a cold heart in a body that God has chosen. We must remember what broke you, and Who put you back together. We must remember what hurt you so bad that you just didn't want to beat anymore. We must remember what has always started that spark again and remember that I have always been a friend. Whatever you feel may work I can help contemplate them with you, I can help you go through the thoughts that you need to go through.

I need you to keep me in touch with what you and others feel, so that I can use my strengths to help them heal. But first, we must work on you and get you back to the place where you had that raging fire.

Because this little flicker isn't working anymore! We were meant to do so much more than this so let the healing begin so we can get on with it. There are people to help and many more things to do. We've got plenty more to learn and it is time for you to begin to yearn for the things that God has called us to do.

I'm here for you because we must work together to make things better. Just know that you'll be fine. So, until next time,

Sincerely,

Your mind

Similarly, anyone who competes as an athlete does not receive the victor's crown except by competing according to the rules.

2 Timothy 2: 5 (NIV)

Rules of the Game:

There are some rules you must abide by if you want to get with a lady like me

You see, I'm not the type who plays that game where you don't have to buy the cow and get the milk for free

I'm a woman who has standards that have to be met and if you don't measure up then that means you aren't ready yet.

Someone like me requires a man who has experienced some things

Who has learned through some struggles and who has endured some life changing pains

You see, I have worked extremely hard to get where I am today, I have lost some, and gained some, but either way there was a price I had to pay

I didn't get to this place by accident or by a lucky chance. I had to choreograph a ballad and to its tune I danced

There was a course that I charted with back up maps just in case. And when it was time to move on or shift I took my appropriate place

The things that I have sacrificed and the life lessons that I have learned. Have taught me how to adjust to this life, you see everything I've acquired, I've earned.

Now what I've been taught along the way is that I am not the only one with requests. Everyone has criteria that must be met, someone who passes the required tests

So now that you know the rules of the game to be with a woman that is sincere and true. It is your turn to layout your action plan for someone like me to win someone like you

IF:

If I had to depart this life today, would my life mean anything?

If today were Judgment Day, what would my existence have to say?

If today I had to return to ash, would my life mean more than just a dash?

...

I would hope my life would signify the things that I believe; not from wealth, and temporary treasures, or the success that I achieved.

I would hope from my life someone would learn a couple of things from me, like love and joy and courage, and always trying to do the right thing

If is the question that one day we all must face, it is something that is in the future but once it passes it cannot be erased.

I don't want to live in a world of 'ifs' but in the world of 'is,' because if it were my last day did I justly live a life that I am comfortable with?

I must do things each day to accomplish all that God has asked of me because the day that I must begin my 'rest in peace' I want know that my soul has truly been set free.

For I know the plans I have for you," declares the LORD, "plans to prosper you and not to harm you, plans to give you hope and a future.

Jeremiah 29: 11 (NIV)

My Future:

Painting an image of endless expression, important?

Ha! It is my passion

Timid at first, from what others may perceive.

But not for long because this dream must be achieved

I cannot be scared of what others may believe.

I'm anointed and this message someone has to receive.

I feel comfort in knowing that this is what I have been called to do.

Watch out now! My future is breaking through.

9-5-02

He hath made every thing beautiful in his time: also he hath set the world in their heart, so that no man can find out the work that God maketh from the beginning to the end.

Ecclesiastes 3: 10 (KJV)

Beauty Marks:

Take a look into the mirror and tell me what it is you see.

Do you see anything that is beautiful there or just tainted imagery?

Look long and hard into your eyes.

Look past all the deception, look past all the lies.

Look past all the hurt

Look past all the pain

Look past all the guilt

Look past all the shame

Look beyond all your imperfections, look beyond all your faults

Glean beyond all the rumors, forget about the insults

Now write down what you find that is beautiful there

Is it your lips, your eyes, your nose, your hair?

Is it the voice of your presence, the tone of your walk?

The strength in your step the soul in your talk

The heart in your touch, the love in your stare

The joy in your smile, the glow of your hair

Is it the fun of your dance, the spirit in your chest?

The song of your heart, the shape of your breasts

Is it the sparkle of your teeth, the twinkle in your eyes?

The figure of your body, the voluptuousness of your thighs

Once you find out the true beauty that is within you, you can stop doing all the detrimental things that you do

You can stop killing yourself through the choices you choose, you can begin to win instead of always having to lose

You can stop settling for less than what you deserve.

You can start trusting in God, the only master that you should serve.

So, now is the time to start discovering the beauty marks that we all have been given.

Take back what Satan has stolen from you and let's get back to living!

Stepping Into Your Future:

Ah look here, they said it couldn't be done

That a kid who started out with so little could end up as number one

But you have found a way to make it, yes, you turned your situation around

Now the pathway to your dreams is beginning to be found

You are on your way now; no excuse can hold you back

Begin to use this as motivation to keep you on the right track

You made a way out of no way and you shut your critics down

Even through all of your struggles the light at the end of your tunnel has been found

So continue to create new goals because clearly you can complete them

Don't let the things the naysayers say make you feel defeated

You took the obstacles that you have dealt with and turned them into stepping stones

You have your head in the game and it's obvious you are in the zone

So, no longer allow your past to control the prospects of your future

Start to consider this as one of the first stitches in the suture

That will begin to heal the hurt and the shame from your past

Finally, delight in this new found victory that you have acquired, at last

No longer be bound by the things you have endured

Continue to fulfill your plans for success so that your potential is secured

You shouldn't forget where you came from because it brought you to this place

Remember to keep focused and work hard so that you can finish strongly in this race

At all times give credit where credit is due

And always remember the people who have been rooting for you

Don't forget to humble yourself and be grateful for this time

Enjoy all your accomplishments because it is now your time to shine

And after showing your appreciation, be proud of the triumphs you have achieved

Because it's time to see fruits of your labor and actually begin to receive what you have always dreamed

Which things also we speak, not in the words which man's wisdom teacheth, but which the Holy Ghost teacheth; comparing spiritual things with spiritual.

1 Corinthians 2: 13 (KJV)

No One Taught Me:

I got caught up in some trouble not so long ago and my charges were increased, because I showed no respect to the officer who arrested me. One thing you have to understand about me is that I was raised in a neighborhood that at one time feared police, but since has turned that fear into hatred. Why would I respect someone who I've been conditioned to disregard, to disdain, and to mock? My P.O. says I should have restrained myself because it would have saved me some trouble, but how can I restrain myself when no one taught me?

On the day before court my lawyer advised me to dress up and look nice. So, I wore my brand new white T-shirt that was still crisp and fresh, my nicest pair of jeans; the ones that sagged the least, and my newest white tennis shoes. Of course I had the hat to set the whole outfit off, but they would not let me enter the courthouse with it on. When I get to court my lawyer looked at me like I am crazy and says "I told you to dress up, why didn't you put on a dress shirt and tie?" I gave him the same look that he had given me, like he had lost his mind, because I knew I was looking decent. I made an effort to look nice I didn't know he was talking about a suit and tie; I don't even own a suit and tie. The only people I know that wear suits are the pimps, the business man, and the man in the casket. Where the hell would I get this so called tie from? Besides I don't even know how to tie a tie; no one taught me.

So, the court session proceeds and I get the maximum because I was rude to the officer and because supposedly I didn't show enough respect for the court through my "lack of concern to dress appropriately for the hearing." At this point I lose my interest in doing the right thing because all the things I had been taught were clearly not good enough for these people. They book me and incarcerate me, and so my days of being locked up begin. After a few months I have a counselor assigned to me; a white lady. How the hell do they expect me to talk to a white lady, she don't know nothing about what I've experienced, all she can do is tell me is a bunch of stuff she learned in a textbook. Oh well, after a few months I get bored to death by being here, so I begin to talk to her. At least, I can hear a female's voice for a little while during our sessions and the more I talked the more she responded. One day, she must have been really moved by our discussion and at the end she came towards me with her arms wide open. I jumped back because I didn't know what she was doing, but, I found out later that she was trying to give me a hug. How was I supposed to know how to respond to a hug, no one taught me?

Being here is ridiculous; you have to take part in the dumbest bull crap. If you don't, you get cut. You can't just be your own person; you have to choose a group to belong to. I was sick of it and one day realized that the religious guys are pretty much left alone. Not that everyone in here is spiritual, but it seemed that by being a Minister or an Imam there is a bit more protection because whether the inmates are religious or not, no one wanted to be responsible for killing a man of the cloth. So, I began to take part in the religious services just to test the waters and see where I fit in. It proved to be very interesting because before that the only Bible verses I've ever heard were at the funerals of my friends and family. The only encounter with Muslims I've had before being locked up was the Muslims who owned the convenient store down the street from us. I used to laugh because they would sell alcohol to everyone else, but if they knew you were a Muslim they wouldn't sell it to you. Anyway, after going to these religious services I kept hearing over and over again that I had to pray, that I had to speak to my Creator, and that I had to make time to have conversations with God. Here again, I am left wondering, how do I speak to God, how do I pray, when no one ever taught me?

At that moment I felt an overwhelming presence come over me and I begin to just start talking. At first I didn't know who I was talking to, but I just talked anyway. In the beginning what I talked about was very generic and simple, but even still it was uncomfortable. Then all of a sudden, the floodgates opened and all the hell that had built up inside of me came out. It wasn't very articulate and it wasn't very polished, but somehow I knew that God didn't care how I said it or what I said but that I just said it. The more I said the more I felt this outcry being guided by something, or someone.

I began by saying, "I don't know how to say what has been going through my mind, but I was told you already know everything about me. I was never taught how to do this so, it is very difficult for me to explain my position. I never had anyone to talk to before about my issues. Those that I tried to talk to either were going through the same things as me and I felt like a punk for bringing up my thoughts to them, or they never experienced anything like what I've been through and they couldn't relate. As you know, I have kept everything that has hurt me, angered me, rejected me, neglected me, and tortured me; locked up inside. It has only proven to be a disaster for me; by keeping things to myself I have become a ticking time-bomb on the verge of explosion. I have become very angry which has only turned into aggression. I have become so use to pain that I don't even realize when I am causing pain to someone else. I have become so detached from humankind that I feel like an alien in a world where I should be able to find a place to fit in. I have become so disheartened that I don't even realize just by the expression on my face how much I am really saying to others. I have become so accustomed to instability that I have lost my hope and expectancy for good things. I have endured so much heartache that has not been dealt with, which has only led to bitterness. I am angry because I didn't choose this life, I am angry not by the color of my skin, but what the color of my skin has cost me. I guess that means I am ultimately angry with you because you created me this way. You chose for me the womb in which I was conceived. You created my mother and my father, and you know them as you know me. You knew my dad would leave me, and you knew my mom would not be able to do it all by herself. You knew all along the way my life would turn out, you knew I would end up here, and you knew the so-called friends I would choose and the things I would do to fill the voids in my life. Because you knew, I am angry. But, in saying all of that I have just now realized that you also knew that it would take all of that for me to find you and speak to you as I am now. All of my experiences and paths that I have taken have all led me to this moment, right here, and right now. Every heartache everything good, everything bad, all happened in an orchestrated fashion to bring me to my knees and fall before you now. As I have come to recognize your plan for me I bring with me a broken heart. Because I know you created me and also broke me I need you now to put me back together. I need you! And because I need you it means that I also need you to lead me in the direction that I must go. I need you to fill in the missing pieces. I need you to teach me. I want to be taught all of the things that I have missed out on. I want to be taught to be kind. I want to be taught to be respectful. I want you to teach me how to deal with all the hurt, pain, and anger. If that means that you must place it in my spirit to know, or if it means you bring people into my life that will teach me; I need to learn and I need to be taught. I thank you Lord for bringing me through to this life changing moment, I am actually looking forward to another day, and I can now feel the heaviness and burdens being lifted from me. I look forward to coming to you more often in prayer and learning about what Jesus has done for me. Thank you until next time.

  Teach me, in Jesus name I ask these things,

  Amen

Scripture Verses Used:

**Bible verses are from the King James Version (KJV) and New International Version (NIV) versions of The Holy Bible.

Book Order Information:

Email Order: smallhousepublishing@yahoo.com

Include:
- quantity
- Name
- Shipping address
- Telephone Number
- Email

Postal Order:

Send Order to:

Small House Publishing
P.O Box 1133
Live Oak, FL 32064

Include:
- The above information for email orders

Payment:
- Checks, Money Orders, Amazon, CashApp, Venmo
- Email your order indicating which way you'd like to pay and instructions will be sent via email
- Please make checks payable to
   - Small House Publishing
- ***Please **DO NOT** send cash through the mail***
- Upon receiving your order, an invoice will be shipped with your order which will serve as your receipt.

THANK YOU,
Your business and support are greatly appreciated!

Made in the USA
Columbia, SC
29 November 2021